The Forest of Wild Hands

UNIVERSITY OF CENTRAL FLORIDA

CONTEMPORARY POETRY SERIES

Florida A&M University, Tallahassee
Florida Atlantic University, Boca Raton
Florida Gulf Coast University, Ft. Myers
Florida International University, Miami
Florida State University, Tallahassee
University of Central Florida, Orlando
University of Florida, Gainesville
University of North Florida, Jacksonville
University of South Florida, Tampa
University of West Florida, Pensacola

For Ellen —with admiration and love —

Judy

The Forest of Wild Hands

Judy Rowe Michaels

University Press of Florida

GAINESVILLE · TALLAHASSEE · TAMPA · BOCA RATON

PENSACOLA · ORLANDO · MIAMI · JACKSONVILLE · FT. MYERS

06 05 04 03 02 01 6 5 4 3 2 1

Library of Congress Cataloging-in-Publication Data
Michaels, Judy Rowe, 1944–
The forest of wild hands / Judy Rowe Michaels.
p.cm. — (Contemporary poetry series)
ISBN 0-8130-2085-9 (pbk.: alk. paper) – ISBN 0-8130-2081-6
(alk. paper)
I. Title. II. Contemporary poetry series (Orlando, Fla.)
PS3563.I3319 F67 2001
811'6—dc21   00-066786

The University Press of Florida is the scholarly publishing
agency for the State University System of Florida, comprising
Florida A&M University, Florida Atlantic University, Florida
Gulf Coast University, Florida International University, Florida
State University, University of Central Florida, University
of Florida, University of North Florida, University of
South Florida, and University of West Florida.

University Press of Florida
15 Northwest 15th Street
Gainesville, FL 32611–2079
http://www.upf.com

For Bill and Terry

Contents

Acknowledgments

The author gratefully thanks Cottages at Hedgebrook and the Banff Centre for the Arts for invaluable support and hospitality during the time when many of these poems were written, and Princeton Day School, which helped fund all five residencies at the Banff Centre, as well as the magazines in which the following poems have appeared or are forthcoming:

CALYX, A Journal of Art and Literature by Women: "Who can tell how a bowl"

Columbia: A Journal of Literature and Art: "Somewhere in the Forest of Wild Hands"

The Journal of New Jersey Poets: "On the Loss of Lemon"

Nimrod International Journal: "Brief Visitation"; "Teachers' Convention"; "You Don't Need Another Cancer Poem"

Poet Lore: "Who Said,"

Poetry: "Lately it's been too much trouble"

Poetry Northwest: "Final Exams"

River Styx: "Taking Cancer on Vacation"

The Texas Observer: "I am my parents' music"

U.S. #1: "Leaving a Loop"

The Women's Review of Books: "Say 'Yes,' People"; "Teahouse Zen"

Yankee: "What We Know"

Tasting the Air

Taste

Ever find a funny taste in your mouth
when you put nothing in it?
Don't tell me about enzymes,
hormones, rhizomes, mangroves, gremlins,
don't spit and rinse please,
no, let your tongue loll
and wet your index finger
to test the air's authority against
yours: Is this childhood leftovers?
satori? last night's conversation
in which the petite blonde asked,
"What's so exciting about seeing a bear?"
and you suddenly felt what's the use
but then wanted to make up bigger
stories to crack the chambre of her
skull and plant flowers in the cranny?
The air says memory count for today
is low, is this a call to prayer, to arms,
the flavor's indescribable, similes dilute
but maybe burnt toast? laundry starch?
there's an arsenic spring north of San
Francisco where the sky's grape-oregano,
but words create endangered species,
taste is fleeting, can't put it on hold,
the mouth's holy, risen,
each invisible grain on your tongue
delivers so many megawatts of
bread, this isn't science exactly
but surrender yourself to cilia,
secretion, salvation, black rain of

silliness in the night, taste comes and goes
east west homeplate, the multi-throat
cultures taken, the many canons
sung to salt, chansons for sweet-sour,
in Gloucester people get injured rolling
cheese downhill, eight-pound cheeses
annually, spectators, cheers and tut-tuts,
baroque cheeses pocked and crusted,
classic creams, romantic cheese maudit—
haunted by blue veins, somewhere the very
pearl of cheese, ensorcelled, waiting
to be kissed, well, doubtless the mouth is
toned by tradition, back in the womb
it was exposed to the best,
but taste visited me this morning
from nowhere, sang canticles to nothing I
knew, where were my standards?
Something's out there swinging on a vine
awaiting commentary, already the day's
risen in my throat and I can't call it by name.

April Inhalation

Today the girlgroup who hang in the nurse's office
to drink cold water from the machine and inhale
all a girl needs to know are leafing out
new tans, bare legs, new brains damp
and curly, a little surprised at how sharp they are.
"How come you always wear hats?"
one asks me, the framing giggles
transparent as air. Oh to just ask
*any*thing, why do you have such long ears,
where did you get your skin, when
do you expect to die and when you rake new grass
and burn it, do you leave gold behind?
I breathe into these pierced ears, noses,
and maybe breasts, how chemo takes your hair
away. Their round eyes make me wonder
where does it go, all the hair
of the world? Icicles, and Spanish moss,
and the comet streaming back every thousand
years, and those clouds we call
mares' tails? The girls inhale my scent of truth,
not quite sense, a perfume they didn't
choose, unlike their leaf-green nails,
ten crowning glories that have stabbed out
cigarettes in the dark, have taken stock
of new hair in strange new
places and point their own way
through the dance of questions
that is the greening of willows
by cold spring ponds.

Reading Akhmatova Translated by Jane Kenyon

Surely Akhmatova wasn't writing for me, a woman
high on Lipton's, snatching passion
from the page between dawn and English IX,
impatient of white space, of memory—*white stone
in its deep well*—of beauty braiding up its hair
for the night. My heart
is the school clock, I can't look back,
can't pause to watch steam rise from
the samovar. Why do we drink hot tea
in summer, even in New Jersey where steam
rises from the tar like a smudged angel?
What can Anna give me while these kids
gather my morning in their sweaty hands?
I gulp the images that Jane, plain country
name, patiently drew from the Russian sounds,
we'd say boiled down, we like to think we speak
down to earth, earth's gold, and Jane died, was it
only last year? The bell will ring for class. Anna is
young, these early poems . . . her lover tries
suicide until she marries him. Still ahead,
a second husband burns her poems in the samovar.
Her work will be denounced,
"useless to the revolution," she will write a poem
for all women who wait in line for news
of prisoned love. All I can see is a door the kids
wait for me to open. Now, in her twenties, she is writing
of the loss of *delectable summer*. Back then
kerchiefed peasantwomen scythed by hand,
the sound, she says, like a hissing snake.
I think she's writing fast, the white field too small
for what she senses of the coming dark.

I mark my place in the poem with one finger
and bring her young heart into class. "Listen,"
I say, "this is what I left for you,"
and I read how she adjures the willow
to get out of her way, how she watches the frozen
lake and writes, *Nothing will happen here,*
not ever.

Christmas Visit

Holidays we sleep incestuously—
you and I in my parents' twin beds,
youngest brother tucked in my old room
enwombed in dusty pink, mother and dad
trapped in two boys' bunks (the absent sons)
out over the garage.
My mother called the figures for this dance.
What shape-shifting in the night,
what trying-on! Their bedroom fireplace
is closed and cold now, where I used to sit
warming my bare feet after nightmares.
You and I play out the reticence
of these pale twin beds, so tightly made.
I get my mother's leg cramps,
your snores swell in tandem with
my restless dream of a death,
a climax, that drives me
down the hall to the old nursery.
How to control sleepwalkers
who follow a sea-green flame
into confusion? This nursery
was always my little brother's, never mine.
Next door I hear him shift in my four-poster
where I dreamed of young men, secret, strong
and cool as hemlock groves. Men knowing
as fathers, but unafraid, unused.
In bunks where two brothers' anger
could not be contained but was thrust away
inadmissible as a mad uncle,
my parents lie, separate but hammerlocked.

Painting the Annunciation

Afterwards there was her clean dress in the sacristy
to shrug into, or if her neck was stiff
from painting *Childhood of the Virgin*
she'd bite the knot and let fall straight down
over her head the dull sheen of obedience
that a young girl wore at home, even in her sleep.

She was learning a craft. Her master was
the man who could make color rush into the virgin's
face, never mind that it might not last.
On gray days the churchlight, thin stream
sent by a single hand to reveal her
to herself, seemed less like a dream

than the hours she spent sewing to please
some unknown man, whose breath she felt
on her cheek sometimes. Then the grand design
of saints, temple, virgin, and a dove
high in the chancel vanished from her
along with the glitter which a man

might almost see if he took the pains. The artist
kissed her once for the way she made Saint Anne's face
turn away, but nights by the fire her mother called her "wild"
when she'd seize a charred stick to draw a shape
she'd seen that day in the arrowing light
of a bare window. Stained glass blurred

one's sight, like a man's whisper.
But painting the child—she wanted
to do that. The master put her off, kept her
focused on the young girl's face. She wanted to make it
look up at the flutter of white, but he told her

the virgin couldn't see the dove. Those feathers

were whiter than sheets, a miracle,
except when light reached a certain window
that threw red toward the dome.
Last week her mother warned her about
bleeding, bound her with clean rags,
which she undid when she got to church

and hung them up with her gown.
Yesterday in the dark she'd seen an angel
glow crimson, she knew what the next frame
would be. She asked to work at night,
to stay alone with torches. She'd move
quietly in shadow, but her mind would see

the whole thing. He needn't outline
woman and messenger, or tell her how
to mix the red, he could go home.
But he set her down before him, her face
turned up to his:
                    "Here is all you need,
this is how she sees the angel."

On the Loss of Lemon

I have lost their word for lemon.
Lemonata? Citrine? Outside they speak
another tongue. We seldom venture out.
When you and I first held our rings up to the light
and saw beyond those jeweled hoops a world
for lovers, green, curled tight as a new fern,
how could we not pass through? We must have shrunk
into ourselves to fit the passage. Now

I have lost "lemon." With a yellow crayon
I could draw one, waxen, lumps at either end.
Look, here on our garden table: citronella,
candle fat melting under a full moon.
Mold me a lemon from that, small, almost embryonic.
O for quartz crystal, pale gold,
false topaz we called it, but it had no seeds.
What falseness is most like? We have lost "lemon,"

just as tomorrow we may lose "melon," "work,"
or "kiss." Don't talk of kisses—small and round
as wedding rings. What I miss most
is rain. Remember, down at the village well
I poured a bucket over a child's head
to say it: "Rain. Have you had any rain?"
I think, despite my pale skin and hair,
they recognized the parched lips of desperation.

Their smiles said "Yes," and shared. If you and I
can talk of rain, why won't it fall on us?
Might it not be the village word for "dry"?
The garden narrows day by day; the market

grows farther off. The loose skin on your cheeks
tightens. Are other pairs in gardens? We may lose
"talk," "flesh," and "bone," till nothing's left.
Today the word was "lemon."

Final Exams

Fourteen, and unlike the deer screened by June leaves
whose death I smell as I pass a certain stretch of woods,
she wears her red heart boldly
on her tee-shirt front, more or less where it ought to be.
Not silkscreened or appliquéd
or embroidered, but genuinely, adolescently
raw, the great aorta bleeding fresh from where
she snapped it off with small, impatient hands.
"A love story is always a descent,"
she writes. The words burst out of the bluebook. "Juliet
dares to die in the dark. She loves so hard
she stabs herself right through the heart. I'd
do it too." (Deer's blood mats the leaves.
Not till the giant crows hover,
will I know where that quick heart died.)
She searched the ranks of the older boys. "Definitely
I've matured. I know what matters now." Ask
whoever is blond and blind and drives the bluest streak,
the one windshield in ten thousand that a bird
flies straight into, feathers, heart, and all.

For My Student Who Said,
"That's For Children"

"I was afraid to write nonsense,"
you said, "I was afraid someone
might laugh."
                        Your hair falls straight
to your waist, you are one smooth
sweep of a potter's hands, tall vase
made to hold water so pure
it reflects nothing but sky,

which is nonsense, as poetry must be.
It mistakes dour for door, cries out
names of the dead and waits a beat
for answers, calls the soul
"seesaw," "poltroon," "dancing
bomb," and sees blind.

Poetry doesn't know any better.
You with your grave eyes and well-ordered
charity, you must forgive it,
try to forget what you know,
let your tongue turn
in on itself and babble about green
skies the color of blood, let your eyes
roll thunder, cigars, white silk
socks.
                        Water laughs only when it meets
an obstacle. I want to hear shining
laughter break out in your hair.

Laughing Falls

We hiked beside the glacier. Late Pleistocene's
hard to remember, but there was a lot more
ice. We argued should we have kids because
hunt and gather wasn't yet a going concern,
his name, well, bankable isn't the term I'd
have employed, and we weren't any too sure
about the sun, it hadn't impacted much. We
did a lot of creaking and howling, that was
the name of the game, if anyone had told us
"lullaby," "thinsolate," "freeze-dry," "down
sleeping bag," we'd have said, "Go climb a tree,"
which was our favorite one-liner, though it
was hard to crack a smile. Ice wine was cheap
and good. Mirrors were easy. Sex was
shiver-and-gully, if you know what I mean,
he'd keep saying *carpe diem,* sun's hotting up,
another ten thousand years this'll be
a lake, then his tongue would freeze to my ear
and we'd stay in that clinch for the next century.
Glacier time had its advantages,
you could develop trust. But we were glad
when the trail came through and the views
diversified. He called my love of flowers
feminine, but that was jealousy. I named
them first, his eyes had gotten so wasted
watching for the next epoch that they couldn't
tell sepals from seeds. He liked abstract,
white on white, elegant, sure, but give me
accents, some dynamic. Waterfalls
took us both by surprise, we'd been pretty
monosyllabic but then one day he starts

to shake—cold? I said—but his mouth
thaws out and kind of curls like a petal,
his nose wrinkles, his eyes squinch up,
it was really endearing, and then this sound
half roar, half bubble, comes out of his throat,
and he kissed me, and I said,
we'll call this laughter.

Marriage

We separate for two weeks. I misplace his chin,
wonder how he manages shaving. Then I lose his voice.
Can he hear himself think? I hope he gives the cat
her pills. We slide in and out of each other's dreams.
He's got my mail, unopened, I have none. He calls for
my license number to pay the parking ticket, my head's
all black light, I can't read numbers, I'm ageless. He
spends my birthday at a theme park but won't tell me
what theme. Do we have control issues? I take long
baths by candlelight and mold words from bread,
what is he reading? A fatherless child finds smooth stones
in the river and gives me some, she tells me about her
dead hamsters. Is he feeding the cat? Your poems
are your children, a woman tells me. Who are his?
For several days he's out of my mind, where is
he? I float in my own dreams like a candle, an egg in
corpselight. When my shell suffers a hairline fracture,
he seeps in. Where do I go? Is this the rhythm method,
forget, remember, time-in, time-out?

Breakfast Under the Mountain

Outside a dog,
a book is a man's best friend.
Inside a dog
it's too dark to read.
FROM RYOZO'S E-MAIL

The Japanese artist and I smile a lot,
we have only two weeks to get acquainted
and there is the work we each came here to do,
fasting all day on solitude and bird cry.
I write haiku—he asks how I manage
kigo. In Japanese there are lists
of birds and weather and phases of the moon to show
the season: *insect song—over winter's garden—moon's
hair thin.* I try to picture Basho on his last
journey to the interior, flipping lists to find
those withered fields where dreams wander on.
In my country, I explain, the children memorize
5–7–5 like a mantra. *Studio chipmunk—nibbles my
best images—grape, bread, cheese, he's gone.*
The artist reserves comment, peels his orange
purely, aesthetically, he is living the juice
of the present moment, which gets in my eye and I see
the old pond disturbed by frogleap.
I wave to our breakfast mountain, almost invisible,
and quote Basho on *not seeing Mount Fuji.* The artist asks
"Please, *'foggy'?*" and we tangle in mist. Aware that this is
a chance in a thousand, I ask about the Formless Self
and "Do you go moon viewing? How often do you climb
Mount Fuji?" I make my hands climb a ladder. No, he prefers

to walk around the bottom. Now he's eating pancake
and sausage. "On my e-mail I have just received
a poem I do not fully understand, maybe you could
help me?" Yes, and I ask him to hike with me
tomorrow, I talk and talk about hiking till he says yes,
he'd been thinking he'd like to try that, but why
do you need special boots to write haiku?

In the Mountains with Ryozo

"Walking *through* the trail," says Ryozo
    as we go up and over the mountain,
and his painter's eye enters a hanging waterfall
    miles off but I see spray on his shirt.
He'll take home Moraine Lake's turquoise heart
    to pierce with crimson flowers.
"Come back, look!" and I turn, slog back up
    because his mind's suddenly gone mushroom.
We're ridge-walking now, and he sees the half moon
    ragged against a clarity of sky.
He says nothing, painting in his head, I think,
    but next day brings me words from the mountain—
"Mind devolved with ridge and sky,"
    says Ryozo. "Deified this side and other side."

He likes the Rockies' vast, embracing light
    that bathes his studio where aspens twirl
right up the glass, their leaves a delicate summons
    to take the air and give yourself to it.
"Most happiest?" he asks me. He fills our lungs
    with blue. Today I'd like to paint
the whole range, even in cloud—Rundle,
    Cascade, Tunnel, wrapped in their river.
We are happy enough to talk death.
    In Japan they pay the monk for death names—
$50,000 respect for a father. His ashes
    will lie still in their box, stacked on more boxes.
Does smaller land mean less sky
    to fill the living spirit, float the dead?
"Happy, most happy," says Ryozo, and we are,
    like the drum that booms within the waterfall.

Moonstone Journal

OCTOBER 10-JUNE 24

October 10

Still dark at the four-way stop, and I drive
carefully, cup the frail egg of fear
between wheel and breast,
don't crack, fear, don't spill, don't leave me
if you do she will die, if you do
I will have to start over,
and suddenly a giant window flares,
ten figures sharp as Magritte
take up position, stretch, bend
one knee, all hitched to music I can't
hear, all so precise in their solemnities
that I wonder if they're awake, or if they know
about the tough fragility of the egg,
how it gleams and sings by moonlight,
how it spins dreams, how
at midnight, for just a moment, it holds
perfectly still, upright, balancing
on some invisible pole that cleaves the heart.

October 12—Student Conference

Suddenly hot, red, wet as fever,
I lean over this young girl's poem—
my chemistry's gone haywire
and hers is just beginning
to make hay. "My mother," she chants,
"with the open heart door,
my mother and I." Her voice is proud,
she's put on words and knows
she looks great: "My mother and I
with our milk flowing necks, my mother
and I with our emerald-chocolate-streak eyes."
She's learning who she is—cloth, color,
and cut. She can't believe
how much she knows. "My mother
with the nose of the fastest dog detective."
Words used to knot and tangle on the page,
but now she combs them smooth
or curls them and twists them to her liking.
"My mother and I . . ." The room's too small
for her and me and words and
mothers. We tear down the walls,
sun and grass give way before our dancing.
My mother leads the way, her dying cells
on fire. "My mother and I," Ali sings,
"with our laughs as sweet as brown sugar on apples."

October 20—"Amazing Grace"

"I'm learning to throw up with grace,"
you said, and I saw reticence
brave as a new white pocket handkerchief
tucked up your sleeve. "En grande dame,"
I teased, remembering our white gloves
to meet God or the city—
and the invisible gloves you wore
to handle love, chickenpox, bloody cats,
mildew, dying love, the knife
in a student's hand. I know the song
but can't decide, in this black twist
of wit and retching, if we've ever met
grace without gloves.

October 22—Fourth Grade Classroom

The children enumerate houses—
igloo, tepee, longhouse, cabin,
skyscraper, shell, cocoon.
"Grave," she says, she is ten
and leads them through the forest of wild hands
to a clearing.
They are thrilled. They are pure vibrato.
How did she think of that?
And I wonder, should we all go back
to "chrysalis," a pretty word,
and what happened to Charlotte when she wove
her sac of spider eggs?
"Grave," she says.
Discovery has so many colors.
Who in here has visited a grave?
I leave it alone, but think how long
a tuning fork will vibrate.
Some day, deep in her own woods,
she will think "house," she will think "grave,"
and go with mop and broom, boxes and tears
to her mother's
in search of a clearing.

October 24

Open a closet to the night
and there's your mother's bedroom,
thump of a suitcase—whose bad dream this time?
You shrink to keyhole level, press your eyes
to the bright hole—she kneels,
lifts a heap of papers from the dark.
"Old banjo notes," she mutters.
You search the stars
but the air is timeless, no weather
here. You say "banjo"
over and over, pass out of meaning
and back again "with my banjo on my knee
sun so hot I froze to death
Susannah, don't you cry."
Is she practicing for death
or just packing?
Familiar exercises both, no need
to hide in closets, but the nights
are full of doors now, and music
rises from the page without
fingers or breath,
what is she hearing?

November 13

He wants to remember, and she doesn't.
She is dying faster, has no time
to grope for breadcrumbs by starlight,
knows the birds were hungry
and there's no trail home.
We children take sides:
he is just being sentimental,
she is strong and unafraid, no,
she is cold, sugarhouse concealing
a dead oven of bones, and he,
in need of sweetness, scrabbles in the ash.
"No, you're wrong," she whispers,
"we went back there three times at least,
maybe four, and the second time it rained."
He hums a crippled tune, can't find
the key change into the bridge, though it's a song
he wrote. She twists her chair to the lamp,
one tough corner to fill in before bed
and she knows all the words.

November 25

You dictate your life
and I write it down
as if we were folding bedsheets
together. An abundance
of warm, white ghosts
to pile on shelves
is what I want,
and to see you
bring your corners up to mine.
You're intent on dates
and the spelling of maiden
names. You want all pain
pressed out—dry lips, sore
fingertips, parched throat,
the struggling breath,
the recollection of old mistakes.
I try to get it right,
and though my draft is a rumpled
mess of crosses and inserts,
your disappointments
remain secret.

If ever, it must be soon, the nights
lengthening, snow in the air,
you eating less than a single bird at the feeder,
wearing a groove in the night as you
try to rock it to sleep in my old
chair, no song for the baby that
snatches your food, your breath,
that won't be stilled. If ever,
it must be soon—a sign in the air,
a shiver of light, a new bird
to lead us through this tangled wood
of mother daughter the way you love
to take me through your photos,
yesterday I misread a bleeding sky
for sunset, it was the only sunrise
you ever took, end of an all-night
journey—quilt, wool cap, pillow clutched to your
breast, light at last over the lake,
climbing the hill path
light breaking down the door.

November 30

It is time to strip you of mother—
see you as I see myself, only leaf
to blaze and die on the mountain,
only child to fall in love
with her parents, firstborn
in her own heart. I should know
the native guide who stumbles
on a spring in the depths of the forest
and keeps it secret.
Whatever thirst she teaches her children,
this wild cold under a rock is
hers alone. I have no child
to teach me privacy,
but today I do up your hooks and see
sheer skin and bone
that I dare not touch.

December 7

I don't know it's the day before your death.
They have tied you into bed, and all I know
is pick, pick at the knots with my useless
bitten nails, suddenly we are two children,
"Quick, before the nurse . . ." Two women
who climbed together in conspiracy
with hawk and rocks and air.
While the morphine takes your words,
drops, breaks, scrambles them till only
touch is left, you shake free
of all restraints but one, your smile
sweet now, the mother you and I
both wanted.

January 24

I take your ring with a difference,
ash turned to water, in which,
if the light is just so,
I see your face, elusive moonstone,
that everyone insists is mine.

If we could start over,
two clear-eyed women, loving our
shimmer and our fear
of sharp tips. If we could lick
saltlight from the other's face.

This ring, his gift to you,
heavy now as the moon is up close
and always on the rise,
I put on. You eye my heart,
checking for what's not there.

March 14

1.

I'm reading the diary you kept at seventeen,
when everything was swell.
An uncle dies overnight and you're certainly
sorry for aunty, but "Top Hat"
plays at the Palace. Your red knit suit
looks smooth, you call your girlfriend
Taylor and ride tandem round the monument
that April trip to D.C. Your mother reads aloud
"The Box of Delights," and there's target practice
with Dad. All boys are decent
or real drips, but it's girls that matter.
Some private anniversary in March,
Taylor—lucky bum, her hair's so smooth—
nearly cuts her hand in two.
Life brimmed with cake and lessons.
Was there ever time to watch
those water flowers you bought in Chinatown
open? Life was Yippee.

2.

You're in college now—apples ripe,
cider and smoke. Today you saddle up
to ride with Taylor. Horses fresh as air,
you've never ridden faster.
You're Artemis, Jo March, dashing
and so straight in the slant sun
that touches up your hair as gold leaves
soften the hills, I'm almost sure

there're no men in your thoughts.
It's all brisk air, crunch, stiff bridle and bit,
a quick crumple of the horse's ears,
exhilaration of riding faster than anyone
till Taylor takes a fall, and at the wood's edge
you must turn back to walk the horses home.

June 24

Your ring is a mountain pond
in thick, gray dawn
where I can't see your face
or even mine. Water weighs
more than we think
gathered in tear or stone.
I was always drawn by the moon

but yours is too heavy for wear.
It sits by me in my purse,
dense, secret. Last night
I took it to a concert
where it drenched the songs
in fishlight, silver shaken from a past
that felt like drowning.

And I think—If I scale myself,
cut right on through,
might the ring be there,
swallowed whole, heavy and smooth
from so much wear I'd know
I hold you hard, as music
once felt is hard to lose.

The Hidden Luminous

Teachers' Convention

There is a moon, and a cow, there is a candle melting
white in a stick, I am jumping thirty-two times
in fluorescent lights amid white-clothed hotel
tables, jumping in a long, blue-flowered dress that I
bought loose to conceal what may be perfectly harmless
cysts, I am jumping to show these teachers how
their kids might jump into calm and poems and remem-
    brance,
I jump out of my moon-eyed, owl-call fear of incision,
of losing babies I never had, I jump out of my mother's
skin and her quick-start cancer, jump through the moonstone
    ring
she left me, I jump with pointed toes, first, and discreet
legs, then come down hard, straight into the floor,
dogmatic and angular, *there are many ways
to kneel and kiss the ground.* Jump, I tell the anxious
teachers, shake the invisible, make the absent chandeliers
tremble and shed their leaves, they are the old
mischief, we must shake them down, jump!

Pelvic

He's doing a pelvic and you breathe, breathe,
waiting for a sharp twist at the roots,
feeling small as a needle's eye, feeling
you are all eye and see nothing but
huge needle finger in a glove. And the nurse
standing firm as a matron of honor
won't try to catch the bouquet because
she knows it all. She says, Breathe,
just as if you might, if you really tried,
give birth to something, oh, worm-like,
tumorous, your slit eye is a desert, it's hard to believe
this sliver was silver once and fresh springs
floated a cool vision, but through your slit
you feel the earth wrinkle, haze, haze, grip,
it's all fade-out, scored
for finger and eyeball, the search
has one flinching center and you, he, you,
will squeeze it dry.

You Don't Need Another Cancer Poem

If you're old enough to drive, you know someone,
you may even wonder about the air,
water tastes odd in the early mornings, what's real?
My bright hair falling, clogging drains, coating pillows.
I'd restored it to the original chestnut with glints
of sunbleached gold, hair is fate, sleep on it wrong
you have to start over, all I know how to do is
brush and brush, my mother's discipline,
she gave me bowl cuts in the bathroom, then
junior high the tight pincurls, little snails,
I wasn't really "out," then jumbo rollers,
I brushed it full of sex and sunlight,
too short to toss but still my one hope.
Now it's like "On the Beach," serious summer
drive-in, where fallout poisons slowly, worming
into the bone, no one quite knew how,
Ava shook out her streaming or is this just how I
remember it, her hair fades on the toxic wind,
forget her bones, my skull shrinks
from nakedness, misshapen? I'm afraid to look,
cradle the last strands in my palm, warm
grass that sprang from the baby's crown,
the woman's glory, I think I know how prisoners
feel, stripped bare for questioning, who are you,
nothing left to thatch and hold the mind
so it won't get lost in this falling air.

What's the Difference Between?

He wasn't supposed to be surfing, he was
meant to find her the very latest the Web had on
ovarian cancer, was it a slip of the finger, a trick
of the eye, that led to *Viola Jokes, part one,*
last modified 1997 / 01 / 03, how many hits it doesn't say,
but these jokes "have been mentioned in such places
as the *Boston Globe,* and *Dave Barry in Cyberspace,*"
they're not some disease that your friends won't talk about,
they haven't slipped silently into your secret parts.
The guy says he collects jokes on
other instruments, too, but viola's the one people
keep sending, the one we're all falling for,
though some of the jokes use medical language
like "brain cell," *How does a violist's*
brain cell die? Alone. Or *What do you get when*
you clone a violist in a hot tub? Vegetable soup.
There are viola jokes with multiple answers,
What is the difference between
a violist and a prostitute? 1) A prostitute has a
better sense of rhythm and 2) A prostitute knows
more than two positions. The jokes detonate
like wet noodles, they lack the zip
of poisonous cures. Yet violists themselves
are violent, *What's the latest New York crime wave?*
Drive-by viola recitals. They're rogue cells playing
off-key, is it dysfunctional families? stress? something
in the milk? It's amazing violists can even
hold their heads high enough for the instrument
to fit under the chin, we are recreating them
lower than the roots of the field, *What is the difference*

between a viola and an onion? No one cries
when you cut up a viola. We must assume violists ask for it,
if they'd just lived right they might be playing
first violin, they might have two breasts, perfect
pitch. Tone-deaf is chronic, they learn to live with it,
What's the most popular recording of the
William Walton viola concerto? Music Minus One.
But the ultimate isolation: *Why do people take an instant*
dislike to the viola? It saves time. And *What's the difference*
between a viola and a coffin? The coffin has
the dead person on the inside.

Household Pet

Keep ahead of Pain, they tell you,
as though that dog didn't know the closet
where his leash hangs on the peg,
as though he won't drag it down,
prancing and pawing till mechanically
you seal the bond, snap and wrap and let him
lead you out across rising
thresholds. You try to slow down
his eager licks, is it love or sweat,
breathe deep, they tell you, today
no one need live with pain. But he
knows where the bones are buried.

No Guarantee

In times of trouble, do you want to
read the words of gods, bake
bread, rub moon juice into your scalp,
hit somebody, or learn the language of stones?
Is this a kind of preparation
for the journey, or do you hope
it will shrink black moon tumors
the X rays just mapped, and melt three doctors'
arguments into one, pure note?
I drink fresh coffee my husband brings in
from the café where I used to write at dawn,
I drink fragrance of white stock and tulips,
the bright, pointy, yellow ones traced in green.
I have washed, combed my dying hairs,
welcomed the nurse changing sheets,
over which the doctors stand disputing.
I count invisible morning stars to find
new statistics, number off flower petals,
I imagine I taste a new drug in the coffee that no one
will yet guarantee, like a moon pit where you might
fall forever or crawl up the other side, gleaming.
We trim the tulips' stems to make them
live a little longer; the coffee's
gone cold. X rays are shadows that grow
in the long afternoons, and where they lead, you follow
into an uncertain twilight, trailing your IV.

Brief Visitation

He says he births people into death,
but he seems gentle, this hospital chaplain,
and he doesn't move in close or insist
on praying with me, instead he notices:
the writing pad on my knees, too many books
for one weekend's infusion. I'm still
on the drips that are meant to defuse,
confuse, generally fuck up, the chemo's side effects,
and I like how he listens, we talk words,
how we love them, especially in the early morning.

I hold up Rita Dove, he writes her down
and says he looks for words to touch
people into love, says he cries easily, sings, too,
but I don't want him midwifing me
away from pain into new life with God.
I *will* him to stay right where he is, half-way
into the room, strong, centered, telling me
how the Bible is a well whose Word
(I prefer words, like *dirt, milk, greed*) finds

and fills him every day. And I am comforted,
touched from my hospital distance, touched to my
wired, drugged, space-invaded core. My breathing
slows to match his and I remember
how my mother's desperate, rasping breaths and my kiss,
the last warm breath she knew, made some kind
of horrible sense. "But not me," my pain is saying,
loud and rude, "not yet, I'm on the rise,
I've got more to say, I'm touched into love."

Hospital

Suppose you die in television noise,
frantic shroud weaving its way from above
your roommate's bed, through the flimsy divider,
to wrap you in marketing?
What were you ever worth, if it comes to that?
A body receptive to cheap music and tumors,
a body that is trying just now to bring all
centers and switches under the control
of a single printed line: *I will die*
on some day I can already remember,
Vallejo hearing an absent rain.
The body's for now, the body exists for
café au lait in the square,
for flooding and tanks, but on TV the tire salesman
is singing about your baby's future.
Suppose you are the baby, each minute
of thought is a milepost, could be the scene
of the accident, which is always tempting
to leave. But it's pure rosewater
to come and go in a book, to remember
tomorrow and feel immeasurably sad, which is just as real
as the TV cooking up new desires.
Now is the moment to look back on death
from under the headphones, buried,
deaf to all but the inner music,
the silenced rain.

On the Shelf

Last week she put herself in the waste basket,
curling her frail spine so she could lick
the tip of her tail. She's all backbone now,
silken but so thin my hand
feels each knob, like Buson's bare feet
stumbling on his dead wife's comb.
She knocks over the basket, now it's a keg
almost drained of cat, she is the lees
my tongue can't coax out.
But this is the space she has chosen, at seventeen
a cat knows something. Next week
she's huddled on the bathroom shelf
between Band-Aids and razors.
Her purr's so slow and deep it shakes her
to her roots and my fingers cold from November dark.

Lullaby

In my dream you blamed me
for never writing poems about sex,
which isn't strictly true, spring froze
the magnolias this year, I wouldn't
mind so much if we weren't married,
my dreams bloom with accusations the color
of pale blood, you said you didn't know
why you should be surprised. Dreams hit
below the belt, I was helpless till I woke
and remembered later to scrape frost
off the rearview window, only glass under there
and in it the disappearing road.
I wrote in the ice, *Slowly she*
stripped to a pink camisole and panties
(I erased panties) and then I revised
the dream.
                    Cancer books like to say
love is more important than sex, but my
mother was saying it long before any of us
thought about dying, she comes to me
mostly in wedding dreams, a silent
witness, but if she spoke it would be
Why do you write so much about sex?
As a girl, my dreams quivered with kisses,
warm wind in the lilacs,
always the same kiss, though the lips
varied, but I wrote lilac and moon
till you kissed me, oh, I guessed we could
make a life out of that, my mother's bushes got so they
blossomed only on top, well above the windows,

now you reproach me in dreams,
what do I want, a body that sings us
awake and to sleep, that lies beside me
writing poems on itself all through the night.

Roadside

Winterstarved, awaiting a sign that is still
weeks off, the beech trees keep their counsel,
dull verticals the same color as deer would be
if a mind could put them there.
Whose mind is strong-mouthed enough
to find browsing yards in a frozen wood?
To make a difference between
shades of brown? The air is yesterday's,
there is no wool on the branches, nothing
has passed this way. My mind
won't clear the fence, just stands by the roadside
trembling. Suddenly an erection
of six, no seven, white tails, a rush,
and the whole wood blooms.

Approaching Chemo #5

You don't want to go back,
you've had just time enough to watch
spring swell the branches.
So dizzying the rising sap,
it's reached the heart, then
Wham! you're back, force-fed
solutions clear as water,
you're vomiting your childtrust in
green seeds on the wind, someone's
cut down the storm-split tree where your dad
rigged a swing, "This is just
hydration," "Now the one that makes you
drowsy," "Now the hard one's going in, just relax,"
and your mouth dreams metal, tastes
dry, tastes retch, you know you'll never
eat again, and you want to smell blue air,
you ask for a shot but you want a nest
very high up where you can creep into a cold
blue egg and not be born.

Taking Cancer on Vacation

When you have a secret, you wonder
if everyone else has, too—why the poolside couple's
bareness matches and they both chose purple
thongs, how the coconuts cling up there in this wind,
ripening, ripening. Yes, we're on holiday
between treatments. I tie up my bald head
in blue and green batik, extravagance
is relative—a little wander beyond
the corner of an eye, and white sails
unfurl. We're out-island, Puerto Rico.
Dark nights here, the bay turns phosphorescent
if you trail your fingers through
invisible waterlife. Moonlight
spoils the show. So does science.
How do these tulip trees keep making
deep orange cups, and why does he still love
to part my lips with his tongue when he knows
how many parts I'm missing, how drugs
and purple scars hold me together? How
extravagant that we can take on trust
the hidden luminous.

This False Sleep

I am my parents' music

but when my father's clashed
against my mother's, I tried
to link arms with quiet, to find it
in the rests, in the blackness
of fast, pounding notes that anger
had lashed together. Their silences were
tight knots in my throat, but quiet
swam with me in the lake at night,
our bare skin slipping through moon-cooled
water, while my parents' music fought
softly from the distant porch.

What We Know

Somewhere a bird is singing upside down.
The child knows her dance will make it rain.
For thirty years my father thinned the wine
with jokes about approaching death. Somewhere
a rainy bird is singing upside down.
A child's talking to the sun. He knows
that fire lives until he puts it out
and when he takes a walk the sun will follow.
The stars are on his leash till dawn, and birds
on every branch are singing upside down
when he spins round and round. My father's pain
slants through the night like rain through evergreens.
Some painters know that black and green are one,
and in their trees the birds sing upside down.

Naturally

we know all about sleep that is practice
for death, our coil goes on losing
its spring till it looks in sleep like the old
doctor's scrawl, no pretense
of tension anymore, well that's what I'd wanted
from his sleeping pill, for five months I practiced
getting lost, but not tonight, I am through with
numb, with blackout, I'll curl tight and loose
as a new leaf, something private between
me and the sky, no capsule
to close me down.
but after two hours watching my watch
I knew something
watched me, not over, not out for, not with,
just eyed me from the lidded bottle,
it was like mind watching itself
and it would stay up all night.
I said, *unfasten the catch, let the boat go,*
I tried flakes of light are falling
through my body, the small nerves
pass them along hand-over-hand,
but there was no dance, no boat, nothing
but the eye, blue and tubular, full of
numbing sleep, and my nerves said,
"here is what we want, give us this false
sleep and we will douse the lights,
return you to the tree, no more watching."
Then I must have slept a bit, for I dreamed
father descending the stairs holding
something, a pill box? No, a tiny thermos,

he sits down at the kitchen table,
unscrews the top, beads of ice, he's just
sprung from the Home, he's free to choose
and he's happy, "this'll do it," he tells me,
he will even share but I hate martinis,
he knows he's safe, and in my sleep something says,
"is this what you wanted? this is your
sleep speaking," so I keep it
simple, on one great
breath I tell my father, "no you
can't, they said no," and my nerves say
"cold" when I knock the thermos over,
gin on green linoleum running free like
rain on leaves, and I wake naturally,
because there is no more to be said,
nothing left that I want to see.

widower

he checks his watch, while the two cats
return again and again to the woodpile,
wanting there to be a mouse, seeing
eyes like pinpricks in black cloth.
the watch is silent but the night
ticks with past and future mice,
small, gray dustballs that flit almost
invisibly from corner to corner,
irregular, as hard to pin down
as moths, a soft distraction at the screen.
he wants her back but if not, he
wants the watch to go faster,
now the woodpile clatters, one cat shoots
across the floor, the other has found hard news
and a tiny leg goes bright with blood,
but they don't know how to
make the kill, and the night ends
with something not quite death
put out the door in an open paper bag.

Who said,

"We learn by going where we have
to go?" I ask my students, who want
to go where they want to go, out
into this too warm, fast budding Christmas

where rose trees are tricked into desire
and my father has just followed my
mother into death and I have faxed my willingness
for his body to go where he willed it.

I'm half awake, my heart is the fire
that wants to take him. How long can it
live off his cold, closed eyes? Magnolia's
in bud now, it will bloom and freeze,

most likely. My students forget what I
know. They are on fire to lose things.
My brothers and I keep forgetting—
we clip articles for him, lift the phone

still warm from last night's call. We want
a white Christmas, we want the buds
to go back to sleep, this strange weather
is just a dream. My students love to tell

their dreams. Suppose we're all asleep,
they say, suppose we're being dreamed
by someone, where do you think we go
when he wakes up? We go out

into this crazy sun. We have to,
who can learn indoors when the chalk
is writing green? My father wakes
to sleep, I take my waking slow.

His and Hers

"NS" . . . "NS" . . . No Sex—for months his journal
whispered this hurt and fury
he was ashamed to tell her. I can't bear
to read. "Where did we lose it?"
he wrote. How Tin Pan Alley, but
I remember, age eight or nine, one spring
opening their door a chink and there she was,
tousled, unpajamaed, laughing in his arms.

"September 5—Lousy summer, no
intimacy, nothing." And it's too late,
she's gone and so is he. Still I can't close
this book where he stripped her
naked. I want to mediate.

Her journal's brisk—meals she fixed, wildflowers,
boating, birds, berry picking. Where is he?
And which was the truer need—"Do you love me?"
Or "Taste this, change your socks." They learned to pass
without touching. Even before death
taught them how.

~ Making My Own Days

When they die, you lose their birthdays,
old mantras—February 10th, March 10th,
this is the first winter I will lose both.
Smoke drifting down chimneys,
maybe a gust of wind in the telephone?
Last year he picked up the wrong end, I shouted
my name, his name, mine, his, until he snapped,
"If you don't know, I certainly don't."
In cartoons when you tear out the phone,
it hits the wall and goes on ringing. And your body
is see-through all the way to the heart, which is weirdly elastic,
inside-out, a raw plaid that matches nothing else you own.
First the ash, then we'll blow out the flame.

Lighting the Bowl

Lately it's been too much trouble

to listen to music.
Alone and young in my Gothic dorm
I'd played Bach and Cimarosa, an old LP,
"The Quiet Door," tasting of cloister
and tea on a hot plate. Bach flavored
the Anglo-Saxon endings, linguistics,
and all of Henry James. Music
opened the morning, brought down night,
but the needle wrote without piercing,
fell gently into the groove,
Kyrie eleison, Lord, deliver us.
Austere, pristine, bowing only
to my Smith Corona, loving the solo
violin, I thought I had chosen loneliness.
Did the grooves deepen? Music survives
our betrayals, the tumors grown in secret,
babies we refused.
I become more beautiful
in your eyes. We almost forget
what we have to, like grace notes
implied, then swiftly left behind
on the way to another key.

Leaving a Loop

Two thousand miles from home, I open a drawer
and—I'd swear it's mine,
the weaving lumpy, my fingers
still all thumbs but they loved the peaceful
push pull pushpull
so much that one summer
on the boathouse porch with the tree growing
right up through the floor
I made thirty-two potholders
on the square-jawed metal loom,
stretching colors soft as old rags
soft as this pale buttercup
this faded-eye blue, and the green
fresh light on maple wings,
seedlight. I wasn't making gifts,
it was the rhythm of the thing,
and the small loom, square and safe,
like the four lines of a child's house.
This was spiderwork, nestwork, easy
till you reached the part where
you unhooked your web from the frame.
Here, see the braided corners? On the last one
somehow you pulled the right thing through
to leave a loop for hanging.
I didn't know I was making gifts
but the winter when my mother died
she still had two, there were stains
and a burn mark, I never thought
of someone's hand feeling
heat through the weave.

Weeding the Cove

Rooting up lilies from the cove, because we don't like
swimming through string and slime and they don't
blossom anyway, my fingers slide down stems
till I reach bottom, but there's no end to secrets,
my blind hand follows a slippery route, thumbing sand
under, over, feeling for when to pull, till finally
there's no more rope and I tug. Up comes a great, dripping
knot, bringing so much lake bottom with it
that my sister says, Rinse it off, let the mud float back
down and settle, but I haul the mess onto a rock
so it can bake in the sun and become the familiarity
of dry land. I never did like to open my eyes under
water, imagined them drowning, washing right out
of their little caves to become lake, watering
the water.
                    Ramifications seem to go on forever—
Whether you wanted us to stay by you longer,
hold you while you fought for breath; if
we'd known it was ending and how it would be to wonder,
month into month, and every summer the cove thickening
with stems that seem to know nothing about their anchorage,
that hold up their green eyes
open wide and free to the summer sun.

On the Sour Sop Tree
in Elizabeth Bishop's Yard, Key West

I'm not at home in the tropics,
but stumble on her gate
and her fruit, grotesque as huge, gilt balls
on a public Christmas tree.
How these pale, scaly moons must sway in hurricanes,
churning with dizzy pulp till
smash, smash, great platefuls
of what I would serrate delicately in a cut-glass dish
slobber the ground, sour sop, sour sop.

Did Elizabeth go out to watch, stand amid falling fruit,
making it at home in her apron
while *lightning made a bird cage of the house*
or was that Brazil? Or Vassar in the rain
with a woman she loved? And where
is the poem taking us now? *Should we
have stayed at home and thought of here?*

I was walking to a gallery, some new artist, the Keys
tumbled and bloomed and drew evening wind
about them, chemo was just starting to take
my hair, and White Street went on forever,
the numbers were going up too slowly, 620, 624:
and here was one of the three homes she lost.
When Valdes painted it, he added palms, a monkey,
a parrot, but not the proud owner,
maybe kneeling in the foreground,
holding a poem called "Home" that tried to
fly upward? She liked his dream so much,
she planted a traveler's palm in that tangled weave

she farmed. A woman there, too, some large, slow mothering
in that place where time seems to pass more slowly,
making itself at home in the wind and water spouts.

Trees I can't count it's so overgrown. Who knows
when she first heard the Cuban women's rich voices
for what they were to her? Poetry roots itself in the dreamer
slowly, it can be sickness or health but settles
into the soil of ancestors, carried over who knows what seas
in the mouth of an extinct bird, on an insect's back.
Slowly the leaves unfold, slowly you learn
to read them, learn to risk the lightning cage,
the shower, the smash of edible and inedible fruit,
to open your arms to a closed gate with a plaque
that asks you if you know when you're at home.

Holy

I lived for summer Sundays,
cold blue ones,
the lake rolling its eyes
like a crazed horse,
wind a triumph in the pines.
We girls wore white—shorts,
shirts. When I sang the hymns
it was a smooth wave rising
to crest silver on the Sunday shore.
I was hooked on hymns, could swim
up from homesickness
to *rejoice rejoice*
casting down my golden
crown upon the glassy
sea. When the lake whitened
and roared, I sang shoals,
sang calms, I put self away,
the cast stones refused me.
I breathed through wind and fire
a balm that was almost
beyond praise,
white Sunday praise.

∼Teahouse Zen

X rays look good, he can feel
no lumps where they shouldn't be,
when I wished for this day I thought
whitecaps, sky on the mountain,
clarity, but now I understand
the fishwife for whom a dress of gold,
a whole palace, wasn't enough.
If you don't know how to be thankful
do they take back the gift,
so you're left alone by a howling sea,
because it could all happen again,
the monthly check-up, the numbers,
my friend met her shadow in a dark
alley, I must write fast and faster,
I must love deep, magic fish, you are drowning,
what I want is the wisdom
of an old woman who runs a teahouse
on a dusty road and nobody knows
why they like to go in there for tea.

~ Who can tell how a bowl

starts to happen, when the curve
blooms, discovers it can hold
water, can accept the grip
of a strange mouth,
thirst's in-drawn music, suck,
swallow and suck,
full falling into empty,
again, again, summer pouring
cold cherries and wine,
autumn the clinging gold of squash,
apples, cream, winter
steaming chicken fat into the stiff,
white air, the bowl spirals
back to its first roundness
of thought or hand, was it someone's
need to remember, or the original point
of light shaping, summoning
an eye? the bowl holds
birth blood, wine dying in the veins
of the old, thrust of a lover's
cry at love passing, ashes and lentils,
the bowl holds
its own beginnings
holds its own

➤ "Say 'Yes,' People"

—for Muriel Rukeyser

"I want to catch for my country," she wrote,
and I thought of Holden, back to the cliff,
arms out to save all errant children,
he catches with his dead brother's mitt, green poems
fading into the palm, how baseball caught us up,
mayors and boys and poets, Muriel
rubs her hands in the dirt, believing a game
isn't over till it's over despite black lung
and black boys hanged on trees, we could put our trust
in the gleam of a rough diamond, nothing
was fixed but everything could be
is how it looks now, when home is the arcade
frenzy of hand-eye alone in a booth
catching no human signals. Muriel guessed
where balls would arc down, back back back
flying west to lift words toward the falling bombs
in Hanoi, running south to the pits at Gauley Bridge
and the dying tunnel drillers, back back,
Scottsboro Boys on trial and the catcher jailed,
sailing back from Barcelona, 1936, running, writing,
catching, forty years in an FBI file, "Every morning
to begin to be nonviolent we must acknowledge our own
violence," running back, eyes on the moving sphere,
she knows the laws of motion, physics of
bat and ball and how the beat of words confronts
the tides of conscience, thrust, thrum, "Do I use
all my fears?" she asked, and I think how a dry well
can fill again with tears for the young and the lost,
but how a loved face gone hollow makes me

flinch. She looked for a meeting place—where
ball finds glove, where heart enters heart enters poem,
and country even with its back to the cliff
embraces the world.

～ AIDS Walk, New York

It's the mothers pushing strollers
I want to know about. Gratitude
for these small bones growing toward
the light, fists clutched on the moving air?
Lack of a sitter? Or a blazing need
to make your child a witness?
Perhaps his veins will remember
this throbbing salsa that rocks the park
as we wait, so many undone by life
but for the moment erect, packed tight,
held shoulder to shoulder to shoulder.
I'm too short to see over the heads—
curled, corn-rowed, bald, wigged—
to where we're going once we're let
go. The baby's eyes follow the balloons,
white, rising against summer blue and green.
I sniff for him, sweat, grass, sunscreen,
grief, and ebullience—we need this
party as we remember bodies
we've cradled, hands that held tight,
then loose, then gone. Babies are
bewildering here, like morning brightness
on the T-shirts whose black lists of names
dance to the sun, and some of us
are dancing, too—that young man alone
with his dead lover. As we start forward,
one slow, sweet surge of blood and rock beat
and the movie cameras, I'm caught
between the Haitian Women's Clinic,
their hair knotted over and over
as if each knot were a memory kept

close, and a prep school group,
serious-silly, their swiveling hips
making the purple banner dip and jerk
like a question mark. Who are we all?
I walk to ward off fear, blindness,
lesions, death—from one whose name
secretly is the rhythm of my walking.
Mother, who wheeled and rocked me,
is gone, I must weave the spells.
Childless like him, I push my fears
over the gravel, follow the baby's round eyes
up toward that balloon held like a blossom
in a dark fork of the spreading tree.

Stop with Me

—for My Mother and Walt

I put my mother on the Brooklyn ferry,
she loves boats, she's okay about
Brooklyn. "Walt, I'd like you to meet
my mother," and he turns his eyes from the kelson
of creation, from the shining music
of the bridge that strings the river.

My mother notes stray grassblades
caught in the loose nest of beard
but she is polite, and he is doffing his broadbrim,
greeting her as *camerero*, sister, lover.
He sees she is troubled. So am I
remembering how she wouldn't vote for

Truman because of his coarse talk, and now
Walt is flinging an arm around her shoulder.
"Stop with me," he cries,
"I am stout as a horse,
affectionate, haughty, electrical, you shall
possess the good of the earth and sun."

My mother, who would hike all day to a sunset,
does not like displays of affection
but inquires politely where he
went to college. "You shall no longer look through
the eyes of the dead, nor feed on the spectres
in books," Walt shouts, his smile is

benign, though the battered hat shakes in his hand
and his hair is wild as the sea.
She backs away toward the rail. He
assures her, "Welcome is every organ

and attribute of me and of any man hearty
and clean." And he belches cleanly, but she

has spotted a new shore bird whose note
is not in her collection of Audubon tapes
and he turns toward her silent watching,
honoring it. For a moment they are one,
they both believe in these winged purposes,
though I know all too soon he will remind her

of how the mockingbird in the swamp never studied
the gamut yet trills pretty well, and she will mention,
casually, her degree from Juilliard, but if he will
just lie back on the deck and loaf and invite her
soul, and not tell her about how much he respects
mothers and the mothers of mothers, she might

extract a small black case and set her mouth to
the silver flute, and her music is parting the shirt
from Walt's bosom bone, lulling them both, till he lifts
his shaggy head and offers the best he can—
"To die is different from what any one supposed, and
    luckier."

Lighting the Bowl

Days when my feet keep the charged globe spinning
faster than they can go, and going
is all the day can do,
I think of a bell caught and held
in the mountains' cold V
under a moon that swells as
slowly as women relinquish love.

To sound the bell seems impossible.
I would settle for being a grain of rice
in a begging bowl.

It's hard to believe
that *when* is unimportant
as crusting moss on bronze.
Marina Tsvetayeva stole to feed her children,
and the youngest died of hunger.
She waited twenty years to hang herself.
In between she loved and wrote and starved.

Saint Catherine died of "holy anorexia,"
in love with the wounds of Christ.
Walking alone in the convent garden
she planned to return the pope to Rome and sang her prayers
hungering for her soul to dwell "like the fish in the sea
and the sea in the fish." Is *where* important?

Shikibu took many men
after losing the love of her life,
but made retreats to mountain temples,
begging the moon to shine in her path,
to light the bowl of her mind.

"I knew myself completely,
no part left out." *Who* is important.

To be the voice of a soul,
the soul of a voice.
Pierced with many notes,
the women spill their music bright as longing
deep as ancient bells
across the world of their encircling arms,
restless and still as the moon
that wakes me.

Notes

"Teachers' Convention": The line "There are many ways to kneel and kiss the ground" is paraphrased from "The Ground," a poem by Jelaluddin Rumi, a thirteenth-century mystic poet. The translation by Coleman Barks reads "There are hundreds of ways to kneel and kiss the ground." See *Night & Sleep* (Cambridge, Mass.: Yellow Moon Press, 1981).

"On the Sour Sop Tree in Elizabeth Bishop's Yard, Key West": Quotations are from Elizabeth Bishop's poem "Questions of Travel," including an allusion to her closing line, "Should we have stayed at home,/wherever that may be?" The phrase "lightning makes a birdcage of the house" is paraphrased from a poem she left unpublished, "It is marvelous to wake up together," later printed in *American Poetry Review* (January-February 1988). All biographical information comes from *Elizabeth Bishop: Life and the Memory of It,* by Brett C. Miller (Berkeley: University of California Press, 1993).

"Say 'Yes,' People": All information and quotations are from Jane Cooper's introduction to *The Collected Poems of Muriel Rukeyser* (Williamsburg, Mass.: Paris Press, 1996).

"Lighting the Bowl": All quotations and information are from *Women in Praise of the Sacred: 43 Centuries of Spiritual Poetry by Women,* edited by Jane Hirshfield (New York: Harper Collins, 1994).

Contemporary Poetry Series
University of Central Florida

Judy Rowe Michaels is artist-in-residence at Princeton Day School and a poet-in-the-schools for the Geraldine R. Dodge Foundation. She is the author of two books about teaching adolescents, *Risking Intensity: Reading and Writing Poetry with High School Students* and *Dancing with Words: Helping Students Love Language.* Her poems have appeared in many journals, among them *Poetry, Yankee, Poetry Northwest, The Women's Review of Books, Columbia: A Journal of Literature and Art, Nimrod International Journal, River Styx,* and *Calyx.*